GU00835893

Key to al-Baqarah

The Longest Surah of the Qur'an

Khurram Murad

The Islamic Foundation

Published by
The Islamic Foundation,
Markfield Conference Centre,
Ratby Lane,
Markfield,
Leicester LE67 9RN,
United Kingdom

Quran House, PO Box 30611, Nairobi, Kenya

PMB 3193, Kano, Nigeria

ISBN 0 86037 270 7

British Library Cataloguing in Publication Data
A catalogue card for this book is available from the British Library

Typeset in Baskerville 11/13

Printed by:
Joseph A. Ball (Printers) Limited, Leicester, U.K.

Contents

Preface

There is no book like the Qur'an. It quickens hearts and transforms lives, it leads whole people from glory to glory. It is the final answer to man's eternal, existential quest. For Muslims, it is the ultimate arbiter of their destiny: be it their rise to the heights of glory and civilization or their fall into the bottomless pits of decay and ignominy, it all happens because of how they live with respect to the Qur'an.

The Qur'an has untold, priceless treasures to offer: the endless joys of blissful conversations with our Creator; the immense riches of knowledge and wisdom that guide on the path of our Lord; the radiant light that illuminates the deepest reaches of souls as well as the most public domains of lives; the healing that cures all our sicknesses, inner or social; the mercy and forgiveness that support, succour and comfort so that we carry the burdens of life joyfully and reach salvation and success both here and in the Hereafter.

These treasures are there for all the wayfarers and seekers. They are available to them *today*, I have no doubt, just as they were available to its hearers *yesterday*, fourteen centuries ago. But the Qur'an has the same claim upon its followers *now* as it had *then*: to hear it and make it heard, to understand it and make it understood, to live by it and invite all others to live by it, to strive to bring human life under the Qur'an. Only then will the Qur'an open its gates for us, only then will it become our destiny.

It is the infinite mercy of Allah upon me, for which I can never be thankful enough to Him, that I have always been granted some share of these treasures – enormous compared to the little I did to deserve them, but very little compared to the vast oceans that the Qur'an has to offer. Out of an urgent sense of duty as laid down upon every Muslim by Allah and His Prophet (bpuh), I have always tried to share with others whatever Qur'an I knew, even if it be one verse. But knowing full well the gross inadequacies of my knowledge and Taqwa, and having no pretensions to being a learned scholar or *mufassir* of the Qur'an, I have always been very reluctant to publish what I have been speaking of. But many friends who heard me have always urged me to make it reach the larger reading public. Hence, this first small booklet, *Key to al-Baqarah*, which, I hope Insha Allah, will not be the last in a larger intended Treasures of the Qur'an Series.

My aim, as I also said in my preface to the *Way to the Qur'ān*, in writing

5

this booklet is very modest. This is not a work of erudite scholarship. I am writing for the ordinary, unlearned seekers after the Qur'an, especially the young men and women, who ardently desire to live by it. I am writing about things which I am learning myself, as one wayfarer to another. Hence the reader will not find here fine points of grammar, lexicon or philosophy, nor rational and philosophical discourses, nor details of *Fiqh*. My sole aim is to make the message of the Qur'an, and its summons to live by it, reach the hearts and minds of readers. Despite my shortcomings, I have every hope that this will rejuvenate them, because I trust the Qur'anic promise: '*We have made the Qur'an easy for reminder.*'

We are living in a time when the need to centre our lives on the Qur'an is most urgent and compelling. Without this we Muslims will never discover our selves, never give meaning to our existence, never find dignity in this world. More importantly, we will never please our Creator and Lord. Without the Qur'an, mankind, too, will continue to slide from abyss to abyss.

What meaning and purpose the Qur'an gives to the Muslim Ummah, how it shapes the Ummah to live up to that meaning and purpose, and what resources of heart and mind, morals and manners, piety and worship, of communal life and institutions are required to fulfil this task – all this is beautifully encapsulated in the 286 verses of *Sūrah al-Baqarah*. The exposition of the whole *sūrah*, though important, would have been an onerous task. Hence I have given a concise overview of the entire *sūrah*, as well as its major themes. I think this will in itself be highly useful. In addition it may kindle an eagerness in the hearts of the readers to reflect upon the *sūrah* in more detail, as well as equip them with keys to undertake that task. In short, it is intended to be a key to understanding *al-Baqarah*, and ultimately all of the Qur'an.

I would especially like to thank Abdur Rahim Kidwai and Sohail Nakhooda, who read the entire manuscript and offered valuable comments and advice. I also thank Sohaib Hasan, Salim Kayani, Abdur Rashid Siddiqi, Abdul Aziz, Batool Al-Toma, Farooq Murad, Ataullah Siddiqui, and Zahid Parvez, whose assessment of its quality and usefulness greatly encouraged me to finalize the work. Whatever errors there are, I alone am responsible for them.

Finally, I pray to Allah, *subhānahū wa ta'ālā*, to accept this humble endeavour, forgive my shortcomings and mistakes, grant me to live by what I say, and not to count me among those who 'say things, they do not do'.

Leicester   **Khurram Murad**
27 Rabiul Awwal 1417
12 August 1996

SŪRAH AL-BAQARAH

Sūrat al-Baqarah is the second and the longest *sūrah* (chapter) of the Qur'an. It has 286 verses, and covers about two and a half Parts (*Juz*) out of the thirty equal Parts into which the Qur'an has been divided to facilitate its regular reading.

Al-Baqarah is placed at the head of the Qur'an; we step into it immediately after *al-Fātiḥah*. Thus, serially, it is the second *sūrah*, but it is *first* in many repects. If we take *al-Fātiḥah* as the preface to the Qur'an, then *al-Baqarah* is its first chapter. If *al-Fātiḥah* is the deepest cry of the human heart before its Creator, outpouring its urgent need and its utter dependence upon Him for being guided to live rightly this earthly life – as it is – then *al-Baqarah* is the first Divine response to that human cry, the first lesson in righteous living, the first step on the Straight Path. And if the seven verses of *al-Fātiḥah* are the seed, the foundation and the sum and substance of the entire Qur'an – as they are – *al-Baqarah* is the first flowering of that tiny seed. And what a flowering! '*A good tree, whose roots are firm, and whose branches reach out towards the sky, giving its fruits at all times by the leave of its Lord*' (*Ibrāhīm* 14: 24–5).

Though placed at the very beginning of the Qur'an, chronologically the verses of *al-Baqarah* were revealed much later, at different times during the Madinan period, so much so that, according to *al-Wāḥidī*, verse 281 was revealed as late as during the Prophet's farewell Hajj (blessings and peace be upon him).

7

Location of *al-Baqarah*

Why, then, has *al-Baqarah* been placed at the very beginning of the Qur'an? Especially when its themes are centred upon the community of the Muslim Ummah and its social life, rather than upon the basics of faith which are prior, and therefore are the primary and dominant concern in the first revelations.

Let us first reflect upon this important question. There must be some reason for it, and the answer should provide us with an important key to understanding the meaning of the *sūrah*. For nothing in the Qur'an is without reason and purpose. Indeed this principle should form one of the fundamentals of our methodology and approach in understanding the Qur'an. We may not be able to answer the question 'why' all the time, or discern meaning behind everything, but it is essential to raise the question at every point.

Two things, however, we must remember while doing so: Firstly, whatever understanding we arrive at, it is very important to always take it as only a human understanding, which is liable to be mistaken, and never to assign it a Divine status. Secondly, no answer should be accepted if it conflicts with the continuing consensus in the Ummah or the overall framework of the Qur'an. With these two warnings always in mind, there should be no harm when we raise the question 'why' at each and every step while trying to understand the Qur'an.

The above question about *al-Baqarah* belongs to a larger question. Why has the Qur'an not been arranged in historical, chronological order of revelation? Why the present arrangement, which has no relation with chronological history? What is the status of this arrangement?

According to some scholars, the *Ṣaḥābah* (Companions) arranged the *sūrahs* according to their own judgement (*ijtihādī*). They could do no better than to make a mechanical arrangement: putting the longest in the beginning, and, in a descending order, the shortest at the end. According to others, it was the Prophet himself (bpuh) who, under divine direction, arranged the *sūrahs* as they are (*tawfīqī*); this arrangement is thematic. I think the evidence conclusively supports the second opinion.

For example, it is authentically reported that whenever a new revelation came, the Prophet (bpuh) told the scribes where to place it (*Suyūṭī*). Moreover, the *sūrahs* themselves had already been compiled in their present form, which too is not historical, by the time the Prophet (bpuh) left this world. Also, he recited them in the Prayers, as well as taught them, in the form and order they stand now. It is also reported that the Prophet (bpuh) used to recite the whole Qur'an during the month of Ramadan in the presence of the angel Jibrīl (*Suyūṭī*). Furthermore, we find that the endings of many *sūrahs* bear quite an obvious thematic correlation with the beginning of the next.

In my understanding there are two main reasons why the Qur'an has been arranged in the present order and not chronologically. Firstly, though revealed at a particular point in time and space, in a particular locale and among a particular people, the Qur'an is Divine guidance for all times to come and for all people. By completely ignoring its historical order, even losing track of it – much to the chagrin and dismay of many Orientalists – it has been lifted out of its particular historical context in time and space and made timeless. Thus it becomes valid and relevant in all contexts. Were it arranged in chronological order, it would have always remained tied to its time and locale. Then it would have become merely an 'event' in history, it would have lost touch with its timeless character.

'Occasions of revelation', however, are there. But they have their use. They help to tell the history behind a specific revelation, where necessary. They also help us to understand it in its context, before we generalize it, or transport it to a new context. But they also tend to root the Qur'an in its own time and locale. For that, we should listen to the renowned eighteenth-century scholar from the subcontinent, Shah Waliullah of Delhi (1702–63). In his seminal work on the principles of *Tafsīr*, he firmly holds that the only valid 'occasion of revelation' for any part of the Qur'an is 'to guide mankind to right beliefs and conduct'. According to him, most of the occasions narrated are not at all necessary to understand the Qur'an, and many of them are of doubtful authenticity as well (*Al-Fawz al-Kabīr fī Uṣūl' al-Tafsīr*).

Secondly, and in particular, while the Qur'an was being revealed, its first addressees were either non-believers, and those who were bent upon denying it, or those who had believed and were being moulded into the desired faith-community (*Ummah Muslimah*). But, after its revelation was completed and the faith-community had been formed, and all denial and opposition – of that time – had come to an end, its first addressee for all times to come was to be the faith-community. For the Book is given into the trust of the Muslim Ummah, which is charged with the responsibility to guard it, to understand and interpret it, to live by it and invite others to live by it. Therefore, at the time of revelation, precedence had to be given to the basic message and articles of faith and to the opposition which the Qur'an was encountering, as well as to the gigantic task of shaping the *muslim* person and the *muslim* community. But, after its completion, precedence had to be given to the faith-community, its purpose, direction, needs and social affairs. This community, which believes in the Qur'an, and derives its identity from the Qur'an, was to be in place for all times to come, and was therefore to be the first to benefit from it.

Viewed in this light, if we look at the contents of *al-Baqarah*, the reason for placing it at the head of the Qur'an becomes quite clear. It also illuminates and helps us greatly in understanding the whole *sūrah*. For we find that in *al-Baqarah* the Qur'an defines the mission of the faith-community, inspires and motivates it, and equips it with all the basic resources and institutions it requires to fulfil this mission.

Excellences of *al-Baqarah*

That is why the Prophet (bpuh) spoke very highly of the many excellences and merits of *al-Baqarah*. Sahl ibn Saʿd reports that the Prophet (bpuh) said: 'Of everything there is a pinnacle, and the pinnacle of the Qur'an is *Sūrat al-Baqarah*. Whoever recites it in his house during the day, Satan would not enter his house for three days, and whoever recites it at night, Satan would not enter his house for three nights' (*Ibn Kathīr, Ṭabarānī*).

Abu Hurayrah reports that the Prophet (bpuh) said: 'Don't turn your houses into graves. Satan does not enter the house in which *al-Baqarah* is recited' (*Muslim, Ibn Kathīr*).

Abu Umamah al-Bāhilī reports that the Prophet (bpuh) said: 'Recite the Qur'an, it will be the intercessor for its companions. Recite the two luminous ones – *al-Baqarah* and *Āl 'Imrān* – for on the Day of Resurrection they will come as two clouds or canopies [full of light], or as two flocks of birds in ranks, pleading for those who recite them. Recite *al-Baqarah*: for in learning it is a blessing, and neglecting it results in great remorse, and only the slothful do not recite it' (*Muslim, Ibn Kathīr*).

To Ubayy ibn Ka'b he said: 'Whoever recites it, on him are Allah's blessings and His mercy. He will have the merit of one who has kept the siege in the way of Allah for an entire year without wavering. Instruct the Muslims to learn the *Sūrat al-Baqarah*' (*Qurtubī*).

Al-Baqarah contains an ocean of meaning. The more one reflects and ponders over it, the more the priceless gems of guidance, wisdom, and more the light that he finds. (A canopy of light, indeed!) Referring to the 'ocean of meaning' it contains, Abdullah ibn Umar once said that it took him more than eight years just to 'learn' *Sūrah al-Baqarah* (*Suyūṭī*).

Central Theme of *al-Baqarah*

Every *sūrah* is a unit. It is an enclosure of messages and meanings, all knit together in a coherent and systematic order, however disparate the contents may look at first glance. Every *sūrah* has a central theme, around which all its contents are woven. What is the central theme of *al-Baqarah*? The central theme, in my view, is the mission of the Muslim Ummah: to state and define it, to exhort, inspire and prepare the Ummah to fulfil it, and to warn and safeguard against any deviation from or abandonment of this mission. This theme is stated in verse 143:

> *We have made you a middlemost, just, model community so that you be witnesses unto mankind, just as the Prophet (bpuh) has been a witness unto you.*

Witnesses to what? To the truth and guidance given by Allah: to Him as the only God (*Tawḥīd*), to the Qur'an as the Divine Book,

11

to the last Messenger as the true Messenger, to the message brought by him (*Risālah*), and to the Hereafter (*Ākhirah*).

Because the Muslim community is born out of *Īmān* (faith), it is a faith-community. Iman means personal, dynamic, total commitment to Allah and His message. It requires giving oneself totally to Allah (v. 208), and to make every sacrifice demanded by Him, even the ultimate sacrifice of life itself. Iman is the identity of the Ummah; Iman is the bedrock of personal and communal strength. Even 'bearing witness' is centrally important only because it is the ultimate demand of Iman. Hence, the theme of invitation to 'īmān' suffuses the entire *sūrah*.

The address is communal, collective and corporate: '*O you who have faith*'. Indeed, nowhere does the Qur'an address a person as an individual. It implies that Iman, by its very nature, must give rise to a communal existence. The addressee is thus the Ummah. Even where a long section (vv. 40–123) is addressed to Bani Israel (the Children of Israel), the primary purpose is to give the new faith-community a picture of what can go wrong with such a faith-community, what diseases of heart and mind, of morals and manners, of conduct and behaviour, may creep in, which may destroy the very foundation and fabric of the community.

Structure of *al-Baqarah*

On reflection, one finds that *al-Baqarah* may be divided into some well-defined sections, all with themes of their own yet inter-related with each other. The sections may be further sub-divided into sub-sections. Such division is not divinely dictated, but greatly facilitates reflection and understanding. According to my understanding, the *sūrah* has seven such sections:

Section 1   Verses 1–39 (39 verses)   Basics of Divine Guidance.

Section 2   Verses 40–123 (84 verses)   Bani Israel, A Muslim Ummah in Decadence: the Broken Covenant and the Diseases of the Heart and Conduct.

Section 1: Verses 1–39   Basics of Divine Guidance

Verses 1–19 describe the type of people who benefit from the Divine guidance, and those who do not.

The *sūrah* begins, very importantly, by declaring its own Divine origin and authority: *'This is the Book (of Allah), there is no doubt about it'* (v. 1). This proclamation we find repeated very often throughout the Qur'an, at the beginning of many *sūrahs* and within the *sūrahs*. Thus the reader moves forward with full reverence, awe, yearning, and a willingness to understand and to submit.

For what purpose has the Book come? To guide. Guide whom, and guide to what? To guide those who are *Muttaqīn*, those who have the quality of piety, God-consciousness, righteous living, or *Taqwā*. Or to guide the intending seekers to become *Muttaqīn*.

The characteristics of *Muttaqīn* are laid out in some detail (vv. 2–5). They need not detain us here. But, it is important to remember that they are the foundations upon which the Qur'an later builds more detailed descriptions of *Muttaqīn*.

This statement – guidance for *Muttaqīn* – is usually understood to mean that only the people who have Taqwa and these consequent characteristics may benefit from the Qur'anic guidance. If this is understood as a necessary prerequisite, then all the characteristics

13

should be taken in their primary, literal meaning, not in the full Qur'anic meaning. Otherwise this would mean that to receive guidance one should be already guided. But, in a sense, this meaning is also true. For the scope for developing Taqwa is endless. To proceed from the primary to the advanced and higher stages, one must have some degree of Taqwa: *'Those who are willing to be guided, He advances them in guidance, and in their taqwa'* (Muḥammad 47: 17).

But a more coherent meaning and sense would be that the Qur'anic guidance will lead individuals and communities to become *Muttaqīn*. Just as when we say, 'this is a course for MA', we do not mean that one has to be an MA as a prerequisite to benefit from the course. What we mean is that this course will lead one to become an MA. Thus the very first verses (1–5) describe how the Qur'an has come to make men and communities *Muttaqīn*. The Straight Path, too, is the life of Taqwa. Later on, we find that a life of Taqwa and its fruits – here and in the Hereafter – are a constant theme of the Qur'an.

As a necessary prerequisite, in a primary, literal sense, Taqwa should mean the innate faculty to differentiate between right and wrong, and the inner strength to recognize and accept the right as right and the wrong as wrong, and to refrain from doing what one believes to be wrong.

The *sūrah*, now, identifies those people who would never benefit from the Divine guidance.

Firstly, there are those who, of their own choice, are bent upon denying the Qur'an as being the Word of Allah. Consequently, their hearts are sealed (vv. 6–7). And, then, there are the people who outwardly claim to have faith, but possess no real faith (vv. 8–20). They are of various categories. At the one end of the spectrum are those who are hostile and mocking, they spread corruption, they have bartered away guidance for error (v. 16). They are hypocrites by choice*: 'deaf, dumb, blind – so they shall not repent'* (v. 18). At the other end are those who have some faith but waver in the face of tribulations and the sacrifices demanded by that faith (*'darkness, thunder, lightning'*) . They are hypocrites by weakness of will and faith: *'whenever it gives them light, they walk in it; and whenever darkness falls around them, they halt'* (v. 20).

14

The *sūrah* now turns to call all mankind to the central message of the Qur'an: 'Worship and serve only Allah, make none equal to or partner of Him' (vv. 21–2). To authenticate this message, it proceeds to establish the authenticity of the Qur'an, and hence that of the Messenger (vv. 23–5). To ground both in the ultimate meaning and purpose of life, it brings home the reality of the life after death (vv. 28–9). In between, the diseases of minds and morals among those who go astray, despite hearing the Qur'an, are also described (vv. 26–7): they question, doubt and dispute the Qur'anic discourse, especially its parables; *'they break their bond with Allah; cut asunder what Allah has bidden to be joined; and spread corruption on earth'* (v. 27).

Thus here (vv. 21–9) we find a lucid summary of the entire Qur'anic message.

Verses 30–9 take up the story of Creation, and thereby expound the Qur'anic world-view and its understanding of the nature of man. Man is given knowledge and free will. He is Allah's vicegerent on earth. He must therefore live within the limits and dictates set by Him. To do so, he faces a continuing struggle to choose between good and evil. Because he is free and morally responsible, he is therefore liable to sin in this struggle. To face this struggle between good and evil, and overcome his sins, he is given two Divine gifts: one, the promise to accept repentance and to forgive sin whenever the sinner turns to Him, as He forgave Adam (v. 37); two, the promise to send Divine guidance, as Allah told Adam (v. 38).

Section 2: Verses 40–123   Bani Israel, a Muslim Ummah in Decadence: the Broken Covenant and Diseases of the Heart and Conduct

Immediately after defining the type of people who may or may not benefit from the Qur'anic guidance (vv. 1–20), inviting all mankind to 'Worship Allah alone, the only Creator and Lord', narrating the Creation event, illustrating the Qur'anic world-view, the human nature, and man's utter dependence upon Divine guidance and forgiveness (vv. 30–9), *al-Baqarah*'s discourse turns to

Bani Israel, the Jews of its time, for 84 long verses, about one-third of its length. It reminds them of Allah's immense blessings upon them, and their ingratitude, their violations of His commands, their major diseases of the heart, of attitude and conduct, of faith and practice. In short, it is a tale of their broken covenant with Allah.

Why does the Qur'an do so? Why does it deal with Bani Israel in its very beginning, at such an important point in its discourse, and at such great length? Let us now reflect upon this important question.

Is it because of the Jewish presence in Madinah? No doubt there were Jews in Madinah, they had to be invited to Islam, and the Qur'an had to deal with the state they were in and with their behaviour towards the Prophet (bpuh) and his message. So this certainly was one of the 'occasions' or reasons for these revelations. But this is not sufficient to explain the length, content and context of this discourse.

Is it because of the Prophet's (bpuh) disappointment and anger at the Jews' stubborn refusal to accept him, and their vehement opposition to him, as many Orientalists often contend? There is no textual or historical evidence to support this contention. The Qur'an is not the type of discourse whose objective would be to vent anger against its enemies, and then put it at its very beginning for all of its readers to observe for all times to come. There is no anger or condemnation here such as we find in the Old and New Testaments. The Prophet (bpuh) went to great lengths to accommodate the Jews, and they were very well treated by Muslims throughout history.

The primary purpose does not seem to be to condemn the Jews of the Prophet's time (bpuh). Rather it is to provide a 'mirror' for the Muslims of all times, to hold up to themselves, to see a faithful reflection of their own condition and destiny. The discourse also delivers judgement upon the Bani Israel because of their failure to discharge their mission, and thus provides the basis to replace them with the new Ummah, the Muslim Ummah, raised under the leadership of Prophet Muhammad (bpuh), to continue Allah's mission.

For, in the Qur'an, history is not for history's sake. Though particular nations have been named, names are mere labels. Their accounts are in fact case studies of communities to show what goes wrong with them and why. From these examples other people should learn lessons.

The Muslims were a newly emerging Ummah, which was being appointed to be the trustee of the Divine guidance, keeper of the mission of all the Prophets, especially the Last (bpuh), just as the Bani Israel had been. Their history had yet to unfold, and any prophecy about future history could not be an example, a lesson, or a warning. People like 'Ād and Thamūd were not Muslims. But the Bani Israel, like the Muslims, had accepted the message of *Tawḥīd*. They, like the Muslims, were charged with the mission of being 'witnesses unto this message'. In fact, they were the Muslim Ummah of their times, but in a state of decay. Their history and conduct was therefore the best case study to place before the Muslims in the very beginning. In this mirror they could see all that could happen to them. The purpose is not to censure the Jews, but to warn the Muslims not to follow in their footsteps. This 'mirror' shows Muslims what can go wrong, where, and why, and the consequences. As the Prophet (bpuh) said: 'You will follow the ways of Bani Israel, step by step' (*Muslim*).

Therefore, though the address is directed to Bani Israel, the real addressees are we Muslims, the trustees and keepers of the Qur'an. Read in this light, the whole 84 verses come to life. They begin to throb with meaning for us Muslims, here and now. Then we find that even specific events of Israeli history, like that of the 'golden calf', become events of our own past and present.

If we look at the section closely, we find that it can be further subdivided into three sub-sections, all interrelated. Looking at it in this way helps us to understand it better.

The first sub-section – verses 40 to 46 – is a general *da'wah* address to Bani Israel. This section provides an invaluable guidance as to how *da'wah* to a decadent Muslim Ummah should be given. It shows what should be the themes and the style, what should be the priorities and emphases. It also gives clues to the programme and process of rejuvenation of such an Ummah. It demonstrates what wisdom (*ḥikmah*) should be adopted in *da'wah* and reformation. Just see how, without mounting a tirade against them, Bani Israel's major weaknesses stand exposed.

The Qur'an first reminds them of the blessing of the Divine guidance given to them, and exhorts them to be grateful for that to Allah. Then, they are forcefully called upon to fulfil their covenant with Him with respect to this Divine guidance. This reminder and call must be the beginning and the bed-rock of any movement to rejuvenate our Muslim Ummah as well. Then it invites them to be the first and foremost in following the path of Iman, because of their claim to be Muslims. This Iman is centred on accepting and following the last Prophet (bpuh) and the Book given to him. Establish Prayers in congregation and pay Alms, says the Qur'an, to mould lives according to Iman. Also, weed out hypocrisy, for hypocrisy is cancerous to Iman. But note the interrogative style – 'Do you . . .' – instead of an accusative: 'You, hypocrites'. Finally, it points to the secrets of strength required to undertake the momentous task of fulfilling the covenant: *sabr* (patience and steadfastness) and *Salāh* (the Prayers). Both can be attained only by remaining ever-mindful of returning to meet.Allah.

On deeper reflection, you will surely notice the striking similarity of this address with the address to the Muslim Ummah throughout *al-Baqarah*. Indeed these seven verses are a microcosm of that more detailed and elaborate address.

The second sub-section – verses 47 to 74 – reminds Bani Israel of various milestone events from their history and their corresponding behaviour. Each event is not a mere 'event', it is a crucial lesson, it deals with some crucial aspect of their life. Upon reflection, each event reveals its lesson, its rich meaning, some major disease of the heart or conduct, or some deviation, which it symbolizes. You will also find that all these events are arranged in a meaningful order, not haphazardly.

Thus, for example, the event of the 'golden calf' stands for love of this-worldly things as objects of worship (v. 51). This event happened soon after the great blessing of Bani Israel's deliverance from the Pharaoh. The Book and the covenant had yet to come. This love, when it competes with and overwhelms the love for Allah, is the root cause of decadence. The rejection of *manna* and *salwā* indicates the rejection of a life of Jihad to fulfil the Divine covenant, which entailed hardship and sacrifices, in exchange for a cosy, comfortable and settled life. Abandonment of Jihad, finally, results in the imposition of 'ignominy' and 'powerlessness' (v. 61). Similarly, the tricks played upon Allah by *aṣḥāb al-sabt* (v. 65), the hair-splitting and casuistry resorted to regarding the commands of Allah, like that of the sacrifice of a cow, are exposed. They amount to the abandonment of obedience and the Shari'ah. Once the Shari'ah becomes a worthless thing, to be somehow evaded rather than obeyed, the inner dynamic becomes static and the hearts become harder than stone (v. 74).

It should not be at all difficult to see how our Ummah's similar abandonment of the Shari'ah and Jihad have led to the similar consequences of subjugation by alien powers (be it the Mongols, or the West), and inner fossilization of hearts.

Verses 75 to 123 – the third sub-section – turn from the history of Bani Israel to their current states of heart and mind, faith and conduct, attitudes and behaviours. Specially depicted is their denial of and opposition to the last Prophet (bpuh). But, it is explained, this is nothing new, it is only a continuation of a long history of such attitudes.

Now take each indictment, each item of the chargesheet, separately, and reflect upon them. You will not only find their key role in the decadence and renaissance of a Muslim Ummah, but also their vast similarities with the states of the Muslim Ummah down the ages. Bani Israel deliberately refused to see the truth and embrace it; so did Muslims. Common Jews became totally ignorant of the meaning and message of the Divine Book, and instead lived in a world of fantasy; so do Muslims (v. 78). Their learned scholars bent and twisted the sacred text to draw meanings which suited their purposes and brought them worldly rewards; so do Muslims (v. 79). Sectarianism became rampant among them, they attached value to religious labels rather than to Iman and righteous deeds; they believed part of the Book and put aside what did not suit them; Muslims are no different. We can go on and on, and we will find the same similarity in every respect.

In the end, the narrative brings us to the final verdict: *'those who do not recite the Book as it ought to be recited, in fact they reject it, they are the losers'* (v. 121).

Section 3: Verses 124–52   Entrusting the Prophetic Mission to the Muslim Ummah

Before entrusting the Prophetic mission to the Muslims (v. 143), an account of the sacred history of Ibrahim, of his godly life, lived in devout and exclusive submission to Allah, is narrated (vv. 123–33). Ibrahim was appointed the custodian of the House of Allah and the leader of mankind because he proved himself in every test that he was put through. He did not receive these honours as an inheritance, and none will (vv. 124–5). The new Ummah is a fulfilment of Ibrahim's prayer as he built the Ka'bah, the House of Allah: *'Raise from our children an ummah, living in total surrender to You (an ummah muslimah)'* (v. 128). Muslims are also heirs to Ibrahim's legacy and mission, the embodiment of his finest traditions of *Tawḥīd* and godliness. It is emphasized that the 'promise' to Ibrahim was not meant to be a title to be inherited and passed on from one generation to another. Israel has forfeited her right to inherit it, for she, unlike Ibrahim, has been unfaithful to Allah. She has failed to discharge the mission entrusted to her by Ya'qub on his deathbed (v. 133).

Great emphasis is laid on the principle that religious labels will be of no avail. Only Iman, self-surrender to Allah, and exclusive and sincere devotion to Him will be of value. Every people will be judged according to their faith and deeds. The whole narration establishes the context for passing on the mantle from Bani Israel to the Muslim Ummah.

The change of *Qiblah* – the direction of Salah – from Jerusalem to Makkah (vv. 144–50), symbolizes that transfer of the Prophetic mission to the Muslims. Just as Bani Israel were reminded of the great favour by Allah to them in blessing them with His guidance and Book, so are the Muslims, at the end: *'Always remember Me, I'll remember you, and ever remain grateful to Me, never falling into ingratitude'* (v. 152). Note the similar call made to Bani Israel.

Section 4: Verses 153–77   Key Personal Resources and the Basic Principles of Din and Shari'ah

Verses 153–62 point to the key personal resources required to fulfil the covenant. They are personal only in the sense that they can be generated only within a person's inner self. But all of them assume a communal shape and infuse the communal life deeply. For example, Salah is congregational, so are Fasting, Pilgrimage and Jihad.

The most important resource is that you remain ever-conscious of Allah, you live in His presence, you see everything as being from Him and because of Him, you remain ever-mindful of meeting Him on the Day of Judgement. In short, you remember Him as much as you can, as often as you can, in every situation and every moment. This much has been clearly stated in verse 152. To achieve this state of existence, Allah's remembrance (*dhikr*) should be integrated in life. The Salah has been prescribed for this very purpose. That is why verse 152 is immediately followed by the instruction to *'seek help with patience and Prayer'* (v. 153).

Patience, or *ṣabr*, is mentioned first. It is because Salah cannot be established and performed without *ṣabr*, whether personal or communal. But it is Salah which generates, develops, supports, reinforces and sustains the quality of *ṣabr*, the quality of resolve, steadfastness and patience. Indeed, both are interlinked in a dialectic process. Both bring the individual as well as the community nearer to Allah. The Salah fills the hearts and lives – both individual and communal – with the remembrance of Allah. Allah is near those who have *ṣabr* as verse 153 promises.

Again, note the similar instruction given to Bani Israel (v. 46).

The stress on *ṣabr* points to the fact that sacrifices will be required to fulfil the covenant. These sacrifices are described in some detail (v. 155). The ultimate sacrifice required is the sacrifice of life.

The key to attain *ṣabr*, in order to remain steadfast in the face of tribulations and other sacrifices, is to remember Allah: to believe that we totally belong to Him and unto Him shall we return, and give Him an account of our conduct. This is what the Salah inculcates.

The verse about Safa and Marwah (v. 158) is not an irrelevant intrusion, even though it may appear to be so. It is placed here because Safa and Marwah – the two hill-tops near the Kaʿbah – both embody a great and inspiring story of *ṣabr*, and hope, and trust in Allah. It is also a story of immense sacrifice: the story of

21

Hajirah and Isma'il. As one walks from one hill-top to the other, one is reminded of how Hajirah – a woman all alone, and with an infant to feed – agreed to live in Makkah, how she strove with hope and trust, and how Allah made water flow in a valley where there was no trace of water.

Finally, the grave consequences of breaking the covenant with respect to the Qur'an are given: curse from Allah, from the angels, from all mankind, and enduring punishment in the Hereafter (vv. 159–62). This poignant warning puts the whole discourse in context. Remembering Allah, Salah, sacrifices and *sabr* – all are essential for discharging the mission entrusted to the Ummah, which each person must do his best to discharge.

Verses 163–77 take up the important foundations of Din and the Shari'ah: faith in Allah alone as God, or *Tawḥīd*, followed by His signs in the universe which inculcate and reinforce this faith (vv. 163–4). Holding fast to Allah is the foundation and substance of Din, of being guided on the straight path (*Āl 'Imrān* 3: 101), the key resource for Jihad (*al-Ḥajj* 22: 78), and the main Truth to be witnessed.

Immediately after *Tawḥīd*, the Qur'an turns to the love of Allah. Love Him more than you love anything else, says the Qur'an. Thus, after remembrance (*dhikr*) and patience (*sabr*), the Qur'an places love of Allah as the most important resource. For, only such love makes Iman real and meaningful (v. 165). Only love internalizes Iman, and gives the strength to live by the will of Allah.

Faith requires obeying and following His Messenger, to the exclusion of all other leaders (v. 166–7). Love too requires fulfilling the commands of the 'Beloved'.

Then come some of the most important principles of Shari'ah. *Firstly*: all good things on earth are permissible, except those things which are forbidden (v. 168). This fundamentally important principle pertains not only to food and drink, but to all things in all walks of life. *Secondly*: the authority to make things prohibited rests only in Allah, and in no one else (v. 169). *Thirdly*: thus only the things prohibited are specified by Allah; the rest are permissible (v. 173). *Fourthly*: the prohibitions can be relaxed in the face of dire human needs (v. 173). *Fifthly*: moral prohibitions are much more important. They, especially when they pertain to duties towards fellow human beings, are not relaxable. For example, the crime of violating the covenant is a much graver sin than eating the forbidden things (v. 174).

However, the foundation of all obedience in life remains Taqwa. Hence verse 177 gives a comprehensive definition of what is Taqwa. This is an enlargement of verses 2–5, and a precursor of the subsequent section. For Taqwa, as defined here is the motive and foundation of all that follows. Iman and *Infāq* (giving away) are also further elaborated here. Abiding by promises and covenants, and patience under all circumstances are the root qualities.

Section 5: Verses 178–242   The Communal Life: Principles, Laws and Institutions

Community life is of primary importance: both to provide the proper soil and environment for the growth and strength of personal qualities, as well as for developing collective strength to discharge the Ummah's mission. Social life must therefore be moulded in Taqwa, as should be the hearts. Hence, in this section, the Qur'an takes up the teachings, principles and laws to develop such Taqwa.

Sanctity of life and property are twin foundations of unity and order in society. They are taken up in verses 178–82. These are immediately followed by instructions about Fasting (*Sawm*) during the month of Ramadan, in order to develop Taqwa or self-discipline to restrain oneself from overstepping and transgressing limits set by Allah in human relations with all 'others' (vv. 183–7). Abstaining from food, drink and sex is not the purpose; the purpose is to develop the inner strength that would enable one to refrain from taking away life, property, (and honour) of others. Hence the command: *'Do not usurp one another's possessions by false means'* (v. 188).

Hajj is linked with Jihad (vv. 196–218). They are similar in nature. Both require us to make sacrifices, to leave homes, relatives, and occupations, to move and travel to reach our destination, and to spend our wealth and possessions. Spending for Jihad, too, is therefore emphasized. Jihad is the key to sustaining the vigour and life of the community, as well as the fulfilment of its mission. Therefore spending for Jihad is necessary to save the community from destruction and decadence (v. 195). Here only the permission for fighting is given, and the purpose of Jihad is explained (vv. 190–2). The discourse then turns to Hajj, and imparts important teachings regarding its salient features (vv. 196–203).

Afterwards the purpose of Jihad is explained in more detail. It is essential for saving mankind from corrupt leaders who wield political power, who are arrogant and refuse to mend their ways, who spread disorder, corruption, and genocide on earth, and bring misery upon people (vv. 204–6).

The need and nature of Jihad and its requirements are laid down. Jihad requires that we give ourselves totally unto Allah (vv. 207–8). Jihad will test us severely and call for great sacrifices. But without offering sacrifices, as was done by muslim ummahs before, we may never enter *Jannah*, or paradise (v. 214). The shedding of blood is certainly abhorrent, but persecution for one's faith and conscience is a much greater evil (vv. 193, 217).

Then the *sūrah* takes up drinking, and gambling (v. 219). Drinking encourages escape from and evasion of worldly responsibilities and toils, gambling induces greed and the urge to make money without toiling for it. Both are evils in themselves, but they are put in this context because they are impediments in the way of Jihad.

The *sūrah* next turns to the oppressed sections of society, to orphans and women. Teachings and rules about family life are given in great detail (vv. 220–42). For it is the bedrock of society and culture. Family sustains social cohesion, and ensures that the objects, values and norms are transmitted from generation to generation. Strong, cohesive and just family life prepares the community for Jihad, too. But it also fits the purpose of Jihad: to establish justice among human beings.

Section 6: Verses 243–83 Jihad (Struggle) and Infāq (Spending): Keys to the Fulfilment of the Mission

What makes nations and communities alive, strong and successful? The last major section deals in detail with this important question. This question is vital in the context of the central theme of the

24

sūrah: the mission of the Ummah. To begin with, it deals with the general principles. Firstly, it stresses that just to have a purpose and mission requires a life of Jihad. Jihad is an active pursuit, striving and struggling for that purpose and mission. Jihad requires making sacrifices: giving away (*infāq*) possessions, especially of wealth and life. Thus Jihad and *Infāq* play a key and determining role in the life and decay, the rise and fall of the Ummah. Both require people to be fearless of death, and to have courage, patience, discipline and to overpower the love of worldly things, especially that of wealth. All these themes are brought forth, with captivating images and inspiring exhortations, in verses 243 to 283.

Fear of death and an overpowering love of this-worldly possessions sap and destroy the strength of a community. If people fear death, then death becomes the fate of their community. Those who have no fear of death, life is their destiny. Verse 243 explains it by referring to an event from the life of Bani Israel. So, the Qur'an summons: 'fight in the way of Allah and give away whatever you can for Jihad. Allah will treat your spending as a loan given to Him and return it with manifold increase' (vv. 244–5).

The fact that even communities in the throes of decline and death may be brought back to life, and kept alive, is illustrated through three stories: the story of Dawud and Jalūt (vv. 246–51); the story of a dead habitation coming to life (v. 259); and the story of the answer to Ibrahim's perplexity in this respect (v. 260).

With *ṣabr* and discipline (keep in mind the earlier narrations about *Sawm* and Jihad), even people, who are few in numbers and meagre in resources and strength, may be victorious against heavy odds, as did Bani Israel, under the leadership of Dawud, against Jalūt (vv. 246–53).

Various aspects of *Infāq*, spending and giving away our worldly possessions, wealth and whatever else may be required to be given for the cause of Allah, are the subject of another long discourse (vv. 261–74). The prohibition of interest and measures to ensure that financial transactions remain free from dispute are related to attitude towards wealth in general (vv. 275–83).

In between is put, like a pendant in a necklace of gems and pearls, the Throne Verse (v. 255). This verse provides all that is needed for the strength of faith in Allah, which in turn nourishes and sustains both Jihad and *Infāq*. You need have no fear of might and wealth of your enemies, nor of losing your life or being poor. For Allah is Ever-living, and the Source of all life. He is Self-subsisting and Sustainer of all else. His knowledge and power extends to everything in the heavens and on earth.

Section 7: Verses 284–6   Conclusion: Moral and Spiritual Resources

What resources give individuals and communities the necessary strength to bear joyfully the burden of living by the will of Allah and fulfilling the mission entrusted by Him?

The concluding three verses summarize these resources. All the essential moral and spiritual resources without which this huge task cannot be fulfilled are given. Only these resources enable us to have the inner strength, commitment, resolve, courage and patience required to live by all that *al-Baqarah* teaches us.

Iman is the most important resource, the source of all other resources. Iman is not mere verbal confession; it is making Allah the centre of life, of all commitments and loyalties, of all fears and hopes. This, in turn, means a deep, strong and all-embracing understanding of, and relationship with Him as the Creator, and as the only Lord and Master. Holding fast to this relationship provides all the strengths and resources to walk the Straight Path (*Āl 'Imrān* 3: 110), as well as for all the struggle in His Way (*al-Ḥajj* 22: 78).

This relationship is given to us here in these three short verses. They are beautiful and inspiring. They are easy to remember and easy to engrave on the tablet of the heart. Let us see what they have to teach us.

Firstly, it is said, remember that *'all that is in the heavens and the earth belongs to Allah alone'*. These few words, once fully absorbed, totally transform all our outlooks, attitudes and relationships with everything in the universe, including with our own selves. They are also enough to generate and sustain all the inner strengths that we require. These words mean:

One, we are trustees, not the owners. Allah is the Owner of everything. Even our lives, bodies, all possessions and relationships, are His – not ours. Keeping this in mind, we find the strength to become His, and to live and behave as we belong only to Him.

Two, being trustees and not owners, we must use everything in life in accordance with His Will. This gives us the strength to obey Him in everything.

Three, everything we receive or accomplish in life is from Him and because of Him. This enables us to remain ever thankful to Him.

Four, this also gives us the patience to face all adversities and tribulations.

Five, being trustees we will surely be called to account for our deeds and misdeeds in things and matters given in our trust. Even what we conceal in the deepest recesses of our heart we shall have to account for. Thus we always keep our eyes on that Day of Reckoning and Judgement, and prepare for the Hour when we shall stand face to face with Him.

Six, it is only in His power, and in no one else's, to forgive our faults and sins or to punish us. This makes us fearless of judgements passed by human beings like ourselves.

Seven, if that Judgement is the final arbiter of our ultimate fate, then we place all our hopes and fears in Allah alone, and turn only to Him for mercy and forgiveness, whenever we fail the test we are put to and commit a sin.

All the above things you will find stated in these three verses.

Secondly, Iman is defined in more detail: faith in whatever has been revealed, in Allah, in His angels, in His Books, and in His Messengers.

Thirdly, Iman is given a concrete shape, it no longer remains only a metaphysical matter. Iman also amounts to a pledge and covenant to 'hear and obey' Allah and His Messenger.

Fourthly, in the face of the gigantic task of living by our pledge and human propensity to sin, we are taught to constantly turn to Him, and seek His forgiveness, both in general, and in particular for all acts of omission and commission. This lightens our burden, this keeps us in a high degree of alertness, self-scrutiny and self-correction.

Further treasures of comfort, solace and support are given to us in the last verse (v. 286).

Firstly, a statement – which is a promise too – of prime importance: Allah will not place upon us any burdens, or put us to any tests, which are beyond our capacity to bear – whether in the obeying of Shariʿah, or in the pursuit of Jihad, or in the making of sacrifices. This exonerates us from whatever occurs in the depths of our hearts so long as we do not wilfully cause it to occur.

Secondly, we shall be accountable and judged only for what we do as a person, and not for what others do.

Thirdly, neither the injunctions of the Shariʿah, nor the trials we are tested with, shall be beyond our power to respond.

Fourthly, we are taught to constantly seek His pardon, forgiveness and mercy in all that we do to live by Allah's guidance. This reliance on Allah excludes any sense of self-reliance.

Finally, we are taught to ask for victory. This again points to the centrality of Jihad in the struggle for carrying out the mission entrusted to the Ummah.

All these teachings are given in the form of a short prayer. What Allah teaches us to ask of Him, He will certainly grant. Without any doubt all these are therefore Divine promises.

Certain Major Themes

We now have an overall view of the *sūrah*. We also know that its central theme is to define the mission of the Muslim Ummah as being witnesses unto mankind, and prepare and equip it with such essential resources – both inner, personal and communal – as it must possess to achieve its mission. If we look more closely at the *sūrah*, we notice certain recurrent themes which interlace the entire discourse and constitute its basis and essence. Let us look at them.

Centrality of the 'Heart'

One, though the focus in the *sūrah* is on the community, *al-Baqarah* puts the *Qalb* – or the 'heart', the inner person, the individual – at the centre of its entire discourse. It is the seat, the cause and the end of all strengths and all diseases. It is the key to the success of all ventures. The *Qalb* is ultimately empowered and responsible for accomplishing the mission and doing all else that the Qur'an teaches its followers to do.

See: There are those who wilfully reject the Truth sent down by Allah. Because of this, ultimately, *'it is their hearts that are sealed up by Allah'* (v. 7). There are those who suffer from hypocrisy. The root-cause of their hypocrisy is that *'they have a disease in their hearts'* (v. 10). There are those who forsake their mission and break their covenant with Allah, like Bani Israel or Muslims. As a consequence, *'their hearts will become hard, they will become like stones, or even harder'* (v. 74). Those who disobey Allah, they disobey because *'their hearts are drunk with the love of the (golden) calf'* (v. 93). Hence they are not moved by the Truth, they do not bow before it, it makes no impact upon them. Similarly, whoever conceals a 'witness', *'it is his heart that is sinful'* (v. 283).

On the other hand, those who deserve to be guided, or who become guided, by the Book of Allah, they are the *Muttaqīn*, those who have faith in the *Ghayb*, the Unseen (vv. 2–3). The Unseen are the realities hidden from human senses, beyond the reach of human perception, beyond any conclusive proof by reason, logic, scientific method or mystic experience – like Allah, revelation, *Ākhirah*, or Angels. They always have scope for being doubted. Iman, faith in such Unseen realities, can only be an act of the heart, for only the heart can take this leap of faith, absolutely trusting the Messenger. Iman can reside only in the heart. From beginning to end, everywhere in *al-Baqarah*, we find this theme of Iman, based on absolute trust in the Messenger. Iman is also the bond that binds and coheres the community and gives it meaning, direction, purpose, strength and identity.

Taqwa is both a prerequisite for, and the end result of, the Divine guidance in varying senses. Next to Iman, it is the most often recurring theme in the *sūrah*. Taqwa, too, is essentially a quality of the heart. It is rooted in Iman: Iman in the attributes of Allah and in Akhirah: meeting Allah, being accountable for life, rewards and punishments. It is this Iman which generates, sustains and develops Taqwa (see vv. 21, 63, 173, 197, 48, 123, 194, 196, 203, 223, 231, 233, 281).

Stress on the Spirit of Laws and Rituals

Two, though the *sūrah* lays down a large number of rituals and legal injunctions, and demands total and absolute obedience, it repeatedly stresses that what is really desirable and worthy and what finds acceptance with Allah is the spirit and the intrinsic dimensions of the outward and formal, ritual and legal acts. Consequently it often decries mere outward religiosity and piety hoisted on empty hearts, and lives which are given half-heartedly in surrender to Allah.

For example: before starting the section on rituals and laws, it is unequivocally declared that 'piety and goodness do not lie in turning to face the east or the west, but in having Iman, giving away one's wealth and possessions, performing Prayers, paying Alms, fulfilling promises and covenants, and remaining steadfast and patient'. Only such people as have these qualities are the true in their faith, only they are truly the *Muttaqīn* (v. 177). Again, it says: *'piety is not that you enter houses from the rear; but piety is to have taqwa'* (v. 169). Similarly, on the one hand, the *sūrah* very importantly directs Muslims to face towards al-Masjidul Haram while praying. But, on the other, it points out that every community has such a physical direction, and emphasizes that hence what makes you really significant and distinct in the eyes of Allah is not to turn your faces in some particular direction, but to *'excel one another in good works'* (v. 148).

In the same vein, the violating of the directives of central importance while rigidly conforming to the peripherals in order to exhibit religiosity, is severely censured. For example, the sanctity of life and property is of primary importance, but here you are, *'killing one another and expelling a party of your own from their homelands'*. And, then, *'if they come to you as captives, you ransom them; so what, do you believe in part of the Book, and reject the rest? Indeed, what else can the retribution for this conduct be but degradation in the present life, and severest chastisement on the Day of Resurrection'* (vv. 84–5).

Similarly, fighting during the sacred months is acknowledged as a heinous crime, but a far more heinous crime, it is declared, is *'to bar people from God's way – and rejection of Him – and [to bar from] the Holy Mosque and to expel its inhabitants from it – that is more heinous in God's sight'* (v. 217). Again, fighting and killing is itself deplorable, *'but persecution is a more grievous sin than shedding of blood'* (vv. 193, 217). Further, if you have to fight, *'never transgress the limits of justice and goodness, God loves not the transgressors'* (v. 190).

Established Religion and Sectarianism

Three, the *sūrah* strongly refutes the commonly-held misconception that merely belonging to an established 'religion' or sect will ensure one's ultimate salvation, irrespective of one's state of faith and righteousness. It repeatedly declares that merely wearing the label of an established 'religion' – becoming a Jew, or a Christian, or for that matter a Muslim – has no value in the eyes of Allah. Thus, whether it be a person or a community, the only criterion by which Allah will judge and recompense them is by the truth of their faith, by their sincere and total surrender and devotion to Him, by their godliness and righteous living.

Sometime people claim exclusive right to *Jannah* on the basis of their 'religious' or 'sectarian' labels: they say, *'none shall enter Paradise unless they be Jews or Christians'.* The Qur'an rejects such claims: *'These are their vain desires.'* Then it challenges them and argues against them: *'Produce your proof if you are true.'* And, finally, it unequivocally declares the cardinal principle of Judgement: *'whoever surrenders himself completely to Allah and excels in good works'* will deserve the reward from Allah (vv. 111–12).

Sometime people claim exclusive rights to be the rightly-guided ones, as if belonging to a particular 'religion' guarantees that one is rightly guided: *'Be Jews or Christians, and you shall become rightly guided'* (v. 135). This illusion, too, is demolished: *'Say to them: No, but*

31

following the way of Ibrahim, who belonged to God alone, and was no idolater [will mark those who are rightly guided]' (v. 135).

It is also commonly believed that even if one belonging to a 'chosen community' went to the Fire, he would be there for only a short while, to be purified and taken out afterwards. The Qur'an counters such a claim by the Jews: *'Have you taken from God a pledge? Not so; whoso earn evil, and are encompassed by their sins, they are the inhabitants of Fire, and there they shall dwell for ever. And those who have [true] faith and do righteous deeds, they are the inhabitants of Paradise, and there they shall dwell for ever'* (vv. 80–2).

Sometime people think that their earlier prophets, too, wore the same labels as they do: *'Do you say, Ibrahim, Isma'il, Ishaq and Yaqub, and the Tribes – they were Jews, or they were Christians? Say: Do you know better, or Allah?'* (v. 140). It is also made clear that the fruits of faith cannot be passed on as inheritance from one generation to another. When Allah appointed Ibrahim as leader of mankind, he asked: *'Is this proclamation for my descendants as well?'* Allah answered him: *'My proclamation does not embrace the wrong-doers'* (v. 124). Then it goes on to affirm: *'They were a people who have passed away; for them is what they earned, and for you will be what you earn, and you shall not be accountable about what they did'* (v. 134).

It is not difficult to see the enormous importance of all these themes in case of an Ummah being entrusted with the Divine mission till the end of time.

Secret of the Rise and Decay of the Ummah

Four, it is made plain in various places and in different ways, that the rise or fall, progress or decadence, strength or weakness, honour or ignominy, that becomes the lot of the Muslim Ummah, depends entirely upon their conduct with respect to the Divine Book and the guidance they are given, and upon how they discharge the mission and fulfil their covenant with Allah pertaining to that Book. The call to the Muslims is the same as was the call to Bani Israel: *'Fulfil your covenant with Me and I shall fulfil My covenant with you'* (v. 40).

Ignominy and powerlessness became Bani Israel's fate because they constantly denied the messages of Allah, killed His Prophets, disobeyed Him and persistently transgressed the limits set by Him (v. 61). Why should the same not become the Muslims' fate, if they too behave in a similar way? The law of Allah in this regard is clearly laid down in verses 159–61.

The Easy Path

Five, it is both stressed and demonstrated that the path of Islam is an easy path. No demand of the Qur'an or Shari'ah is beyond the power or capacity of man: *'Allah does not lay a responsibility on anyone beyond his capacity'* (v. 286). *'Allah desires ease and not hardship for you'* (v. 185). In all injunctions this principle is found to be observed: e.g. eating and sex are permitted during Ramadan nights; trade and business is allowed during a Hajj journey; exemption from fasting is granted to the sick and the traveller; mutual consent and harmony in family life is enjoined.

This aspect is also the basis of the key principle of Shari'ah laid down in the very beginning. All things are permissible, except those explicitly prohibited.

Empowerment of the Individual

Six, while the *sūrah* lays down considerable injunctions in almost every sphere of life, very significantly at no place does it specify a punishment for the violation of any of these injunctions. Rather, we notice from the text a quite different approach. While laying down an injunction, everywhere the Qur'an touches the heart, enlivens it and makes it responsible to obey. It fills hearts and minds with a consciousness of Allah: that we are totally dependent upon Him; that He is with us, seeing and hearing; that unto Him shall we return; that we shall have to give Him a full account of how we lived, that on His judgement depends our destiny.

Thus the Qur'anic methodology is clear: to make the individual responsible, and to empower him to do what is required to be

33

done. For compliance of Allah's will and His commands, it trusts his innate conscience, rather than punishment.

Social Life

Seven, the *sūrah* throughout lays great stress on developing a strong and cohesive social life. It links the requirements of such a life with the ritual worship. Thus, for example, after laying down detailed injunctions about Fasting, it immediately proceeds to say: *'But devour not one another's possessions by wrongful means, neither bribe the authorities so that you may sinfully and knowingly devour any part of another's possession'* (v. 188). More importantly, there are no relaxations in respect of inter-human relations, like those given in respect of forbidden foods or obligatory acts of worship.

Jihad

Finally, we must take particular note of the continuing emphasis on Jihad (spending lives) and *Infāq* (spending of wealth) for fulfilling the mission that Allah has entrusted to the Ummah, and on the sacrifices required for this purpose.

Only by commitment to this purpose and goal, and actively, devoutly, and dedicatedly striving for its achievement, can the Muslim Ummah ensure honour, dignity and progress for itself in this world, as well as *Jannah* in the Hereafter for Muslims.

Further Readings

For those who desire to study the entire *Sūrah al-Baqarah* in more detail, the following readings are suggested. As few expository works are available in English, works in Arabic and Urdu are also included.

On how to study the Qur'an

— *Way to the Qur'ān* by Khurram Murad, The Islamic Foundation, Markfield, Leics., UK.

On *Sūrah al-Baqarah*

— *Towards Understanding the Qur'ān*, Vol.I, by Sayyid Abul A'lā Mawdūdī, tr. and ed. Zafar Ishaq Ansari, The Islamic Foundation, Markfield, Leics., UK.

The English version of *Tafhīm al-Qur'ān*, Mawdūdī's monumental commentary in Urdu. By far the best short commentary available in English.

— *The Qur'an and Its Interpreters*, Vol.I, by Mahmoud M. Ayoub, State University of New York Press, Albany, NY, USA.

An excellent source book. Ayoub lets the major *mufassirīn*, down the ages, themselves speak on *al-Baqarah*, mainly the classical Ṭabarī (d. 310/923), Ibn Kathīr (d. 774/1373), Wāḥidī (d. 468/1076), and Qurṭubī (d. 671/1273), the rational Zamakhsharī (d. 538/1144), and Rāzī (d. 606/1209), the sufi Ibn 'Arabī (d. 638/1240) and Nishāpūrī (d. 728/1327), the shi'i Qummī (d. 328/939) and Ṭabrasī (d. 548/1153), and today's Sayyid Quṭb (d. 1386/1966).

— *Tarjuman al-Qur'an*, Vol.2, by Abu Kalam Azad, ed. and tr. Syed Abdul Latif. Asia Publishing House, Delhi, India.

An interpretive translation with short comments, it provides some useful insights on the *Sūrah*, as well as on the methodology of understanding the Qur'an.

— *Tafsīr-ul Qur'an*, Vol.I, by Abdul Majid Daryabadi, Academy of Islamic Research and Publications, Lucknow, India.

A very useful short commentary, rich in references from the Bible and classical *mufassirin*, especially Thanawi's *Bayanul Qur'an*. Also available in Urdu.

— *Muwadhdhah-e-Furqān*, by Mahmudul Hasan and Shibbir Ahmad Usmani, Mujamma' al-Malik Fahad, Madinah, Saudi Arabia.

A very useful short commentary in Urdu. The translation follows Shah Abdul Qadir's classical work.

— *Tadabbur-e-Qur'an*, Vol.I, by Amin Ahsan Islahi, Furqan Foundation, Lahore, Pakistan.

A detailed commentary in Urdu relying mainly on the Qur'an in interpreting it, offers some deep insights. Should be highly useful.

— *Tafsīr al-Qur'ān al-'Azīm*, Vol.I, by Isma'il Ibn Kathir. Dar al-Fikr, Beirut.

A standard classical work in Arabic.

— *Al-Jāmi' li-Ahkām al-Qur'ān*, Vol.I, by Muhammad al-Qurtubi. Dar al-Kitab al-Arabi, Cairo.

A comprehensive work in Arabic.

— *Fi Zilāl al-Qur'ān*, Vol.I, by Sayyid Qutb, Dar Ihya al-Turath al-'Arabi, Beirut.

Most widely read contemporary work, dealing especially with the literary and movement aspects of the Qur'an.